# What is Maths?

Tracey Steffora

**www.raintreepublishers.co.uk**
Visit our website to find out more information about Raintree books.

**To order:**
☎ Phone 0845 6044371
🖷 Fax +44 (0) 1865 312263
🖳 Email myorders@raintreepublishers.co.uk

Customers from outside the UK please telephone +44 1865 312262

Raintree is an imprint of Capstone Global Library Limited, a company incorporated in England and Wales having its registered office at 7 Pilgrim Street, London, EC4V 6LB – Registered company number: 6695582

Text © Capstone Global Library Limited 2012
First published in hardback in 2012
The moral rights of the proprietor have been asserted.

Edited by Daniel Nunn, Rebecca Rissman, and Harriet Milles
Designed by Joanna Hinton-Malivoire
Picture research by Elizabeth Alexander
Illustrations © Capstone Global Library Ltd.
Originated by Capstone Global Library Ltd.
Production by Victoria Fitzgerald
Printed and bound in China by Leo Paper Products Ltd

ISBN 978 1 406 22902 8 (hardback)
15 14 13 12 11
10 9 8 7 6 5 4 3 2 1

**British Library Cataloguing in Publication Data**
Steffora, Tracey.
    What is maths?. – (Acorn plus)
    1. Mathematics–Pictorial works–Juvenile literature.
    I. Title II. Series
    510-dc22
A full catalogue record for this book is available from the British Library.

**Acknowledgements**
We would like to thank the following for permission to reproduce photographs: Alamy **p. 7** (© STOCKFOLIO®); © Capstone Publishers **pp. 14, 15, 18** (Karon Dubke); Getty Images **pp. 12** (Tooga/The Image Bank), **13** (Andersen Ross/Stockbyte); iStockphoto **pp. 5, 22 top left** (© Stacey Newman), **10, 22 bottom right** (© Lauri Wiberg); Photolibrary **p. 17** (Richard Hutchings); Shutterstock **pp. 4** (© Alexander Chaikin), **8** (© Nick Stubbs), **9** (© Alfred Krzemien), **11** (© Sophie Bengtsson), **16** (© auremar), **19, 22 top right** (© pixshots), **20** (© Stephen Coburn), **21, 22 bottom left** (© PeterG).

Front cover photograph of a) coloured pencils reproduced with permission of Shutterstock (© djem), and b) simple maths witih permission of iStockphoto (© Hande Guleryuz Yuce). Back cover photograph of a young girl counting red apples reproduced with permission iStockphoto (© Stacey Newman).

We would like to thank Patricia Wooster for her invaluable help in the preparation of this book.

Every effort has been made to contact copyright holders of any material reproduced in this book. Any omissions will be rectified in subsequent printings if notice is given to the publisher.

# Contents

Some words appear in bold, **like this**. You can find out what they mean in "Words to know" on page 23.

# What is maths?

There is maths in everything we do. There is maths in everything we see. How many yellow vans can you see in the picture?

Maths is a way we understand the world. Maths is all around us.

# Maths is shapes

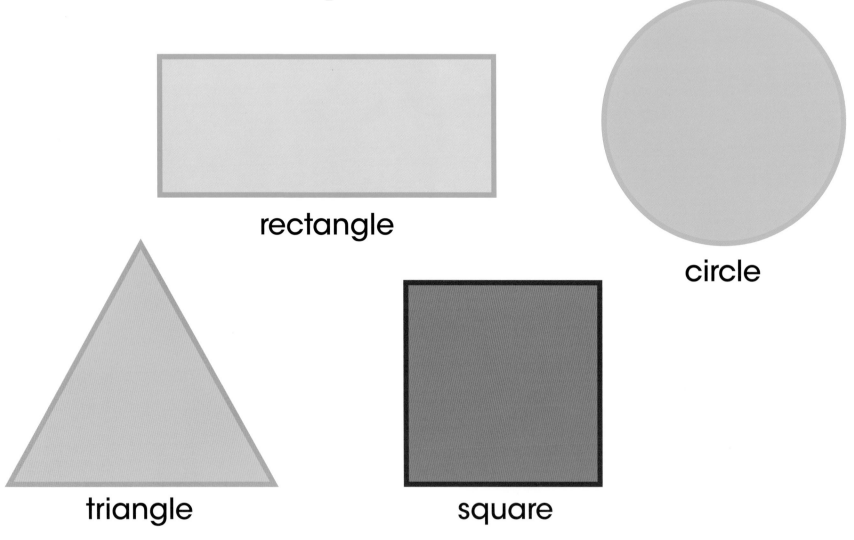

rectangle

circle

triangle

square

Everything has a **shape**. Some shapes have special names. Squares, rectangles, triangles, and circles are examples of shapes that have special names.

side

corner

Shapes can have sides and corners. Shapes can be big and small. You can see shapes everywhere you go. What shapes can you see in this picture?

# Maths is patterns

Sometimes things have a special order to them. This order is called a **pattern**. A pattern can be things in a row that get larger or smaller. A pattern can be things that **repeat**.

Numbers can be a pattern. **Shapes** can be a pattern. Colours can be a pattern. There are patterns everywhere you look.

# Maths is sorting

When you **sort** things, you put them into groups. We sort to help us organize and find things.

There are many things we can sort. We can sort things by colour. We can sort things by size. We can sort things by **shape**. We can sort things by how they are used.

# Maths is counting

Sometimes it is important to know how many there are of something. We **count** things to find out how many there are.

Numbers help us count. We can count many things. Counting happens all around us.

# Maths is adding

When we **count** more of something, we are **adding**.
This person is adding eggs to a cake mixture.

# Maths is subtracting

**Subtracting** means taking something away. When we subtract something, we have fewer things left. If we take one cake away, how many will be left?

# Maths is measuring

scales

Do you ever want to know how much there is of something? Do you ever want to know how tall or how heavy something is? Sometimes we use **scales** to help us **measure** how heavy things are.

thermometer

Do you ever want to know how hot or cold something is? Measuring can give you the answer. A **thermometer** can measure how hot or cold it is outside.

ruler

Sometimes we use special tools to measure.
This girl is using a tool called a **ruler** to measure
some flowers!

Sometimes we measure by **comparing**. We compare things to see if something is bigger or smaller.

# People using maths

People use maths at school and at work. This man is **measuring** the wood he needs to build a house.

People use maths at home. This cook is measuring oil to put into food.

# How do you use maths?

How have you used maths today? Where do you see maths around you?

# Words to know

**add**  count more of something

**compare**  we compare things to see if they are different

**count**  we count things to see how many there are

**measure**  we measure to find out if things are tall, short, big, small, heavy, or to find out how much of something there is

**pattern**  happening in the same order

**repeat**  something that happens over and over again

**ruler**  tool that helps you measure how long or short something is

**scales**  tool that helps you measure how heavy something is

**shape**  the outline that something has

**sort**  put things into a particular order

**subtract**  take something away

**thermometer**  tool that tells you how hot or cold something is

# Index

## Notes for parents and teachers

**Before reading**

Show the children the front cover of the book. Ask them if they can see anything around them that shows maths. Explain to the children that maths is all around us through shapes, numbers, counting, and in many other ways.

**After reading**

• Fill a plastic bag with different types of coloured shapes, and give each child one bag. Ask them, "Are there different ways to sort these shapes?" Some possible answers may be: by size, shape, and colour. Ask the children to pick one way to sort their shapes, and explain to a partner why they sorted the shapes in the way they did. After they have sorted the shapes, introduce some addition and subtraction exercises. For example, they could add up squares plus triangles, or red shapes plus blue shapes.